The afterlast English Letters

Ulla Renner, geb. 1950 in Finkenbach-Gersweiler, arbeitet als Übersetzerin für Englisch und Französisch. In ihrer Freizeit betätigt sie sich als Hobbygärtnerin und spielt für ihr Leben gern Lotto.

Ulla Renner

The afterlast English Letters

Die hinterletzten Englisch-Briefe

Illustriert von W. P. Küttner

Eichborn Verlag

CIP-Kurztitelaufnahme der Deutschen Bibliothek

Renner, Ulla:
The afterlast English letters = Die hinterletzten Englisch-Briefe / Ulla Renner. – Frankfurt am Main: Eichborn, 1986.
ISBN 3-8218-1877-8

 · Cover: W. P. Küttner · Gesamtherstellung: Fuldaer Verlagsanstalt GmbH · ISBN 3-8218-1877-8 · Verlagsverzeichnis schickt gern: Eichborn Verlag, D-6000 Frankfurt 70

INSTEAD OF A FOREWORD

My dear Mr. Director:

Please do not wonder why I write you this letter. I will sit you in the picture very quickly.
I'm writing this letter very slowly, because I cannot read so fast and that you can understand it better.
I tell you, I am a poor devil (more poor than devil). And because I am poor, I have no money, and because I have no money, I cannot play Lotto, and if I don't play Lotto, I cannot win money, and if I cannot win money, I have no money. I am really a poor devil . . .
So I thought I write a book. A short one. Because too much work is too much stress. And I don't like stress!
For the moment I send you only a few stories so you can make you a picture from the other stories I want to write.
If I break my head a bit more, and if I write my fingers bloody, I can send you the other stories quickly (30 stories nonsense in 2 or 3 months or so). Is this nothing?
With this book I want to make the big throw, you know. And as I am always heavy on wire and never on the woodway I'm sure you will make my book a hot bestseller.
Don't throw it away!!! The paper has cost me 3 cigarettes. If you do not want to read it, max nix. Just print it and read it after it is printed. And when you have read the 8th edition, you will take me out for a work dinner, yes? Don't be afraid because of the money, I don't eat and drink very much. And besides, you will get the money back from your company. –By the way, I don't like Bratwurst!!!

don't like the dinner we can then talk about my second book. Is this nothing? You will make a lot of money. I will make a lot of money and can play Lotto. Everybody will be happy.
I await your quick answer. You know: Time is cash!!!
I greet you kindly. So long.

P.S. I was going to send you a picture of me, but I had already sealed the envelope.

Indianer-Häuptling an Hausverwaltung

To White Face:

Hugh, I Häuptling Sleeping Foot.
You give me new Wigwam.
New Wigwam nix good. Squaw Silly Chicken not happy.
Make fire on bottom for cooking.
Big hole in bottom. Fire fall down in Wigwam of other red brother.
Other red brother angry, because fire fall on his backside when he make little red brother.
I want smoke peace pipe. But he make war dance.
Red brother in Wigwam under him angry. Too much noise.
Cannot understand drums from red brother under him.
He make smoke signs to Manitou. Manitou nix hear and see.
Already sleep.
Smoke comes up in our Wigwam.
I want old good Wigwam!!!
If not I take my **horse Sleeping Pill** from roof and come tomorrow with my Tomahack and make you new hair-cut.

Hugh, I have spoken.

When I was born!!!

When I first saw the light of the world, I was still quite young (9 months or so). When my father saw me first, he was from the socks, because I had so many folds in my face and on my backside.
He could not find out what was face and what was backside. So he was very sad and told my mother to send me back again and to make a better one.
My mother was a bit more than stinky and said: "Now make it half-long and do not flip out. Look at this beautiful baby. It looks like an angel, because it comes after me."
But my father said that he had never seen an angel with so many folds, with sail ears, with no teeth, with no hairs on the head and without wings.
These were the last words he said on that day, because my mother knocked him out with the bed pan.
When we left the ill house, life was normal again. At home, I had my own room, 6 meals per day, regular cleaning of my lower region and a lot of free time.
After a few days, my voice was already on full power. 90 db (A) is nothing against it. And after two weeks, all rats and cats of the neighbourhood had wandered out. I was the hero of the street.

My first School Day

My mother always told me that school is a very fine thing. I really believed her.
But after my first school day, I knew that she must have been mad when she said this. School??!!! Forget it. You know what school ist? The most unnecessary thing since Adam and Eve.
The best of my first school day was my school bag with the negro kisses and the candies.
The first minutes, the teacher was very nice, but when all the parents had gone, he made a sour face and told us to shut up.
He was already very old; twenty-one or so. Black hair with a lot of grease, ears like an African elephant, poison-green eyes with thick glasses, a hook-nose, square mouth, yellow teeth like our neighbour's horse, double-chin, arms like a monkey, O-legs and shoes like a violin case.
And absolutely no humor. He gave me one behind the ears just because I wanted to find out the effect of the wonderful brown negro-kisses on the pink wall.
And when he had cleaned his trousers from the 3 negro kisses on his chair, he said to me: "Go in the corner and shame you what!!"
And this was the place where I spent most of my school time.

Brief eines türkischen Arbeiters an Wohnungsamt

Dear Mister!

I want you plies giv me and my wive and 4 boys and 2 görls other aprtmend who has more rooms.
Now liv in room where coocking, sleeping and drinking. This maks health of body ours kaput.
When come of night wörk to apartmend, I nix can sleep day and night, bicause children mine olways cry. I can not make the eye close bicause neybour mine beside my apartmend knocks on his wive day and night.
Two beds from us are at wood wall. Oven direct beside bed. I always so hot that I burn. And nail from picture in wall sticks in popo mine when sleep.
Dear Mister, and then I want, you come and see kloo which is dangerous because soon fall through bottom, bicause bottom is stink-foul.
Allways we stand in shit with one leg. Room much too small. And nix good when children see when make traffic with my wive and when neighbor looks through hole in wall in our bed and stick in my ass with long stick with nail.
Plies come look, but only three bicause room too small and give me apparmend with more rooms.
Excuse I write so bad. I come from night wörk and must sit on kloo because my wive wash upper body hers on table.

With greet from Turc worker.

Kündigung an Arbeitnehmer

(Dear) Mr. McKilroy:

We are very sorry to say, but we have to separate us from you.
Our patience with you is at the end. We cannot more.
You make us fix and ready.
We understand much, but what you make with us, is under all pig.
We understand when people come sometimes too late, because they sleep too long or that people stay at home sometimes for the one or the other important reason.
But what make you?
You come too late every day.
And the excuses you find out in your never-ending phantasy knock the bottom out of the cask.
One time you say the coffee was too hot to drink quickly.
This is so a stupid excuse that there comes us the cold coffee high.

One time you say your canary has the flu and that you had to measure the fever and make cold compresses. When we hear such a cheese, then goes us the hat high.

And your dog must be a special intelligent animal. Because every third day you say that this genius has drawn your bus ticket out of your pocket and hidden it and that each time it takes you hours to find the ticket.
Do you think we have a screw loose or what? We know that you live only two minutes from here!

But your very best excuse is your grandmother. She has died at least 15 times during the last six months.
And now some words on your work which tears us not from the chair. Your work consists of coming too late, drinking coffee and tea, singing dirty songs, walking around and disturbing people and telling them dirty jokes, reading sex magazines and making dirty offers to our secretaries.
Therefore, we think you should pack your plastic bag and make a fly!

KÜNDIGUNGSSCHREIBEN AN ARBEITGEBER

Dear Sirs,

With this letter I want to say you that I have the nose full from your company. I throw you the battle before the feet. This can you not make with me, you know. I, Herby Doodle-Bag, tell you what! You can stick you your whole company into your . . .!
I do not let me sell for stupid. I'm not fallen on the head! (not that I remember).
And if you think you can make this with me, then you are heavy on the woodway. You know what I mean?
You always shout with me. I cannot understand it.
You shout if I come too late a little bit. What are two hours per day?
You shout, when my early-piece takes only a few minutes more than two hours. I need that time to eat my butter-bread and to drink my Muggefugg.
And it is quite normal that I must relax after the early-piece.
And all these telephone calls. What want all these people from me? I cannot help them. I am here to work and not to telephone. The only important call is from my wife when she tells me what to buy for dinner. And this talk ins only 30 minutes.
And when I have opened my table and taken out all my papers, it is already lunch time. You can say what you want, but I need at least two hours for lunch, because I cannot eat so quickly, and it is not so good for my stomach.

Ja.

Wir verstehen uns, im besten Sinne, als »Publikums-Verlag«. Weil wir Bücher machen, die wir gerne mögen.

Literatur und Sachbuch, Bildbände und Satire. Aktuelles und Klassisches, vom Nonsens bis zum Tiefschürfen. Das Programm ist so bunt und widersprüchlich wie wir selbst.

Genau betrachtet, sitzen wir zwischen allen Stühlen (und fühlen uns dabei sehr wohl): Linken sind wir nicht links und Grünen nicht grün genug, Konservativen viel zu links und zu frech, Intellektuellen nicht intellektuell und Weltverbesserern nicht pädagogisch genug. Na undsoweiter. Weil wir es niemandem recht machen wollen.

Wir sind neugierig. Aufmüpfig. Unbequem. Wir finden nichts schlimmer als Langeweile. Mögen nicht die Weltuntergangs-Larmoyanz. Wir wollen Bäumchen pflanzen. Und auch noch Spaß dabei haben.

Neugierig geworden?

Dies Kärtchen lesbar mit Absender versehen, frankieren und zur Post. Dann kommt unser Verlagsprospekt, »Querkopf« heißt er, und erzählt mehr über unsere Bücher.

Ja, ich möchte den Verlagsprospekt gern haben.

Meine Anschrift lautet:

____

____

____

Eines unserer Lieblingsbücher:

Hier wird das komplette Alte Testament rasant runtererzählt. Mit Spaß und Spannung, »Sex and Crime«, für Christen und Nichtchristen. »Dieser unheilige Knüller« (Münchner Merkur) »fasziniert wie ein Gute-Nacht-Krimi« (Die Zeit). Der neue Weg zur alten Bibel, 848 heitere Seiten lang. **Nur 16,80 DM**

Eine Leseorgie!

Eichborn Verlag
(, der mit der Fliege)

Sachsenhäuser
Landwehrweg 293

D-6000 Frankfurt am Main 70

And you always shout when I relax on the lying chair after lunch. I think this is not very social from you.
After my midday-relax it is already coffee time which is until 4 o'clock only. You cannot say that this is very long. There is still half an hour left to put all the papers back and to close my table.
And all this day for day, week for week, month for month, and only six weeks holidays per year, and only 2 weeks ill per month.
And this for 5 years now!
No, my gentlemen! This stress is too much for me. My wive says I am already a nerve bundle.
Now you can look for another stupid. I take my hat and go! I have already found a new job which is not so stressy.
I am going to be test-sleeper for double-beds.

I greet you!

Your Herby Doodle-Bag

P.S. They even pay me for over-hours!!!

Brief Enkel an Opa

Hello Oldy!

You must help me. I am down-burnt. The cheque from father is not yet here. This is perhaps a shit life as a student. Never have you money.
You know that I bought me a Suzuki. 500 cubic. 100 horsies. Really, a hot oven! When I come next time, we two will make a trip to the town. The machine makes 230. This is not from bad parents. You will like it.
We can draw us a beer in the head and tear some girls up. You can have one of my stone-washed jeans. Then you look like Rocky in person.
Can you send me 500 fleas? You have so a high pension, 500 Marks is nothing for you.
I have a new Pussy. The heart would go you up. She looks like Brigitte Bardot in old days. Do you remember Brigitte Bardot? There runs you the water in the mouth together, what?
I will show you the night-life of today. You will never forget it. As long as you live.
Don't wait so long with the 500 Marks! My Pussy-Cat costs me a lot of money. She is sharp like a potatoe knife! See you later.

Your Freddy

P.S. Hearty luck-wishes for your 85th birthday. I give you a beer out when we are in town.

Brief Enkel an Oma

Dear Grandmother:

I hope that it goes you good and that you feel not so bad. What makes your Zipperlein? Don't work too much. You are my best grandmother and I want not that it goes you bad.
Grandmother, I have a problem.
I have not yet the cheque from father. I hope that it comes soon. But in the between-time I have no money. I could only pay the rent for my room.
And now I have nothing to eat. And how can I study and work with an empty stomach which is always knurring like a little wolf.
I have a new girl-friend now. She is very nice and very shy. And she is from a good house.
You would like her.
And now I have not a penny to buy her a few goose-flowers. Can you send me perhaps a little bit of money? Only for bread and butter and for a few goose-flowers.
Oh, nearly I forgot.
I have an angle-hook in my trousers. Can you send me a little bit more money?
So much for today, little grandmother. I must go and study now. The whole night. Because I want to be the best of the students, you know.
Please write me soon.

Your Freddy

Antwort Opa an Enkel

Hello Freddy:

Thank you for your letter.
It is really a cross with you. Never have you what druff.
That must you have from me. When I was young, I was a do-not-good like you.
But is was wonderful. Yes, yes, the good old times. When I saw your grandmother first, I was from the socks. She was a real flowerly-touch-me-not-on. Everything was quieter. Not like you and your bees and your machines.
But I must tell you, I like this time too. When I sit behind you on your hot oven and when the wind blows me around my ears and curls. This ist not null-eight-fifteen. This is a bomby feeling. And when we tear the girls up, I feel like in 5th spring.
When you come, you must go with me to the Waikiki Bar like before 5 years. They make perhaps a stripptease!
Vow!!!
But I want to sit in the first row because my eyes are not more so good. And when I have seen everything, I will show your grandmother how to make a flotte spripptease. Normally she stripps herself only in the dark.
And after the bar, we go to the Disco to swing the dance-leg, yes. But one I can tell you. With Rock 'n' Roll and Disco-King is it out. My rheumatism makes me a line throug the invoice. Last week I had a witch shot.
This was not so good.
But I hope it is better when you come.
And then we make the streets unsure. Vow! How I like it!!!

Perhaps we can also go to an massage saloon.
I send you the money you want. But please remember the next time that 50 has one null and not two.
Wait not so long. I become not younger.

Your Grandfather

P.S. Don't tell your grandmother that I have sent you money. And nothing from the Waikiki Bar and the massage saloon!

ANTWORT OMA

My dear Frederic:

Your letter was really shocky!
You poor boy.
Nothing to eat!
And so much work.
This is really terrible. Like in the second Worldwar.
Today I send you a field-post-packet with liver-sausage and pig-stomach. And with this letter I send you 150 Marks. Give them not all out.
You know the speakword: Save in the time, so have you in the misery.
Send me your trousers that I can flick the angle-hook.
I am very glad that you have a new girl-friend. The other one was nothing for you.
She was so ordinäry. And already so old. And she said always you to me.
Don't work the whole nights. This is not good for you. You need your sleep.
It max nix when you are only the second best.
Please don't tell your grandfather that I have sent you money. I took it from his pension. He has his money in a green saving-sock in a plastic bag in the water box from the closet. He knows not that I know.
It is really a good idea to buy goose-flowerlies for your girl-friend. Your grandfather gave me forget-me-not when we were young.
He is a little bit through-another in the last two days. His eyes

are glitzering and when he stands before the mirror, he makes to funny figures.
I think he becomes now slowly a little bit calky. And he has cut his hair. Have you words! He sees out like Mecki.
Terrible.
When we go on the street I do so as if I don't know him. He hears simply not on me. When you come next time, speak you a serious word with him and tell him that he is not more in the puperty. Perhaps he hears on you.

Many greetings

from

Your grandmother

Ostfriesische Mutter an ihren Sohn in USA

Dear Son:

Thank you very much for the bottle mail. Please do not forget the stamp again next time.

Your father said you should better send a bottle with whisky instead of a bottle with letter, because he can better drink than read.

I write this letter very slowly, because I know that you cannot read very quickly.

Have you found a good work?

Please do not say so dirty words to your boss. He will not like it and fire you.

We have winter now and it is very cold.

Don't forget to draw you warm undertrousers on.

And draw your cap up. And wash your hands after the meals.

Don't use fork and knife too often, because it is not good for your face. The last time, you had to stay in hospital for two weeks.

Yesterday, there was a terrible accident near our house. A mini crashed against a tree. 5 deads and 8 wounded.

Your sister Ottilie has a baby since today morning. I haven't found out whether it is a boy or a girl, so I don't know whether you are an aunt or an uncle.

On Thursday, your father was overolled by a truck. Now he is in hospital.
Room Nr. 104 to 107.
I hope you have a nice room to sleep. With no rats and so.

On Wednesday, I bought some coffee, and half of the coffee was rat-shit. I wrote a very angry letter and sent the rat-shit back to the coffee company. I cannot help, but the coffee has still a strange taste.

Now I say good bye. Keep your ears stiff and write me back very soon.

Your mother

P.S. I was going to send you some East-Friesian Dollars, but I had already sealed the envelope.

SOHN AN MUTTER

Dear Mother:

One I can tell you. America is great! My dear Mr. singing-club! There are so many new things here I have never seen before. I feel very fine, and I have already had several jobs.
First I worked in the kitchen of a big restaurant. I helped the cook to make mirror-eggs, apples in sleeping skirt, pomm fritt and steam noodles.
One day the cook was ill, and I had to cook alone. This was the first day when I saw people with green-yellow faces. And it was the last day of my cooking career.

In America, dogs are very poor animals. Because at every corner you can buy and eat hot dogs with bloody sauce. I could kotz if I think of it.

People are very clean here. They wash at least once per day. Isn't this crazy? They must have a wheel off. Too much washing is not good for the skin you have always said. Therefore, I wash me as usual, once in 4 weeks. But what I cannot understand: people always make a large curve around me.
But there are also people here who are brown or even quite black. I think they have never washed themselves in their whole life. But nobody make a curve around them. Really funny!
The have very high houses here with special drive chairs. I went up and down 20 times. Then the meals of 4 days came out.
I have a very nice double-room with so many new things. In the second room I can make rain. I have still not found out what it is good for.

Besides, I have an automatic washing machine in this room, but it is not working very good. Yesterday I put a shirt and three socks in, then I pulled the chain and everything was gone. Now, I'm very afraid to wash my lousy head in it, because I fear that it goes down the pipe, too.
Mother, imagine, the little animals I have in my room are the same as in East-Friesland. I feel like home.
Goot bye. I wait for your bottle mail.

Your Son

P.S. I miss your lion tooth salad.

Mutter an Sohn

Dear Son:

I'm very glad that you are fine and that you feel at home with the little animals in your room. Me goes it not so good today.
I have a bit headache. Yesterday, your father was blue and in his delirium he thought he was Willy Tell. He wanted to shoot an apple from my head. With the empty Whisky bottle. He hit directly below the apple. This afternoon I'm going to make him apple pie and coffee. With rat poison.
Two weeks ago, your uncle Herbert died from liver shrinking. He had a beautiful death. He had drunk 5 bottles of Vodka before he threw the spoon away. His body was burnt in the crematorium. It took us 3 days to put the fire out.
Last week we had bad weather. It rained only two times. First for five days and then for two days.
Thank you for sending me the 20 Dollars. We are going to buy a new house on the beach. And the rest we put on the bank.
The day before yesterday, your brother spent 5 hours in the refrigerator before we found him. He wanted to find out, whether the light is really going out when the door is closed.
I put some lion tooth salad with the letter in the bottle. It will surely stay fresh in the water.
Now be a good boy and think of your mother.
If you don't know what the rain in your room is good for, why don't you plant potatoes?
Please write me soon.

Your Mother

P.S. Don't smoke in bed; the ash falling down could be your own!

SOHN AN MUTTER

Dear Mother:

Thank you for the lion tooth salad. It was quite good. Perhaps a little bit salty. And oily. The bottle was half open.
Me goes it good. But yesterday I got a great shock. These people here are cannibals!!! Imagine, mother, they eat Hamburgers! And Frankfurters! Please tell Aunt Luise not to come over! It would be too dangerous. I don't want to eat her on the bread.
On Saturday I was in a dancing hall. They call it Disco. I made me very fine for this. Red Shirt. Green trousers. Warm long under-trousers. Yellow tie. Blue and black socks. Butter in my hair. Cowboy hat. And my good black nailed shoes.
It was really great in that Disco. Vow!! Many girls. You know I dance good. I swang my dance leg with a nice blond girl.
After 20 minutes they threw me out. They said I had hurt 12 people with my nailed shoes. This is too high for me.
I have never hurt people with my good nailed shoes. You know that. Next time I go with my house-shoes. On Sunday I was the first time in the church here. I tell you: Once and never again. In don't like this bloody God service her. It is not half to funny as at home in East Friesland. They are so stiff. Only sitting on the bench and singing and praying. The Pastor speaks only from God and Jesus. He does not tell jokes as our Pastor at home. They play not 17 and 4, they sing no dirty songs, they dance not, and they have no beer there. This is nothing for the son of my mother. I must finish now. I have pressure on the bubble. Make it good. Greet your man and my brother.

Your Son.

MUTTER AN SOHN

Dear Son:

You are me parhaps one. When you forget the stamp on the bottle again, I give you one behind the ears? Have you shit in your head or what!
You have nice letter paper. Please send me some.
Yesterday, the Jehova people were here. They told me that the end is very near and that the world would go under very soon. This was perhaps a shock for me!
Your father asked them what it gives to drink in the sky. They didn't know.
So he said he would go to hell and make up a whisky burnery with your Uncle who died from liver-shrinking. He has already packed his suitcase and is now sitting on the beach and waiting for the happy end.
I hope it goes you good. How are the girls in America? Have you already a girlfriend? If you have found one and you do not know what to do with her, then write me. I will tell you. It has something to do with bees and flowers.

The last 4 weeks your father had a fine job. He had 400 men under him. He was cutting the gras on the church-yard. But they fired him again because they found 40 empty whisky bottles on the graves.

Last week our neighbour died. I cannot understand why. He didn't drink, he didn't smoke, he didn't work, he didn't do the things with the bees and the flowers. That cannot go good.

HIER RUHT IN FRIEDEN

He had a great funeral.
The people applauded half an hour, and they had to pull up the coffin 10 times.
Your father was the star. He danced the Eastfrisian “Bottle Rock”.
Behave well that you come in the sky when the world goes under.
Don’t draw you too warm on when the world goes under because they say the great fire will come over us.

Many greets!

Your mother

Brief Sohn an Mutter

Dear Mother:

Don't shout with me. I made the stamp on the bottle. Really. Perhaps a fish was hungry and has eaten ist. I know why. I had no Uhu and therefore I took orange marmelade. And fishes like orange marmelade. I know from our gold-fish at home.
Yesterday I had toothache. I went to the dentist. He said my mouth looks like a bomb-crater. He had to draw one of my last 4 teeth. When he came with the long needle, I gripped his eggs and said: "We do not hurt each other, yes?" This afternoon I visit him in the hospital. He has a very funny voice now. So high. Like a girl. Really funny! Last week I had a very fine work. I was newspaper-boy. Early in the morning I brought the newspapers to the people living in this district. But on Thursday, the weather was very bad and we had a cloud-break. So my boss said: "No newspaper today". My dear Jolly, this was perhaps a work to go to all the people and tell them that they get no newspaper on that day because of the bad weather!
I have not found a girlfriend, but when I find one, I write you.
The automatic wash-machine is no wash-machine. I found out that people sit on it and make their small and large business. Very practical. And they do not take grass to clean their ass. They have special paper hanging on the wall.
But you can also use this paper as letter paper. I send you a roll. But it goes not in the bottle. Perhaps I make it around the bottle and then you can dry it on the line.
Make's good.

Your son

Brief Mutter an Sohn

Dear Son:

Much thank for your bottle mail. This time the stamp was on. Brave boy!
What makes your toothache? Is it okay? I hope you have not hurt the dentist too heavy.
Thank you for the writing paper. It was not so much. Perhaps some stinky fishes have used it to clean their ass. Send me new one next time.
Your father is still sitting on the beach and waiting for the end of the world. 3 weeks now!! And he is drinking like a hole. Bottle for bottle. Day and night. I think he is more drinking than waiting.
Yesterday I collected the empty bottles and brought them back to the super-market. From the money I got I can live like God in France the next 3 months.
Many people come to see him. This stinks him. Therefore he ordered me to paint on a white bed-cloth: Off limits! Every third will be shot down. The second was just here!!!
Now he is alone again. And he stinks miles against the wind. Because he is sitting in his own shit. You know what he said yesterday? Every day blue is also a regular life.
My dear son, I tell you what: marry, and you laugh you dead!
So much for today. I make me a bed bottle, then I shoot the lights out and go in my bed. Good night.
Behave you.

Your mother

Brief Sohn an Mutter

Dear Mother:

Thank you for your letter. Tell father that the Jehova people are liars.
They lie like printed. They lie the blue from the sky. He should better lift his ass and go home. I think he has a wet cheese in his pocket. Yes, yes, the suff reibs the people uff. Give him the Hucke full, perhaps it helps. I think someone has shit in his brain.

I cannot sleep the last days. In my bed there must be hundreds of wood-worms.
They work the whole night. Must be very hungry. They make perhaps a noise! Crtsch, crtsch, crtsch. One day my bed breaks together. Shit worms.

Tomorrow I buy a few books and lay them beside the bed. Perhaps they like more to be book-worms. Then I bring them to the bookery. There they have enough to do, and I can sleep again.
I have a new job since yesterday. I am at the police. They gave me a fine uniform. When I was there yesterday morning, they asked me only one question: Who killed Jesus? I didn't know. So they sent me home again and told me to after-think.
Mother, imagine, one day at the police, and I have already a murder at the neck.
This is unfair. They have the not all on the Christmas tree. But I will show them. I will find this stinky murderer very soon and

they will look like an ox when's blitzt. I am not so stupid as they look.
I send you some letter paper around the bottle. Some of it I have already used on the kloo. But I think it will be clean when you get it.
Now I make me a bread with 3 onions and then I go to my wood-worms in concert. I show them what real music is.

Your Son

P.S. Press me the thumbs that I find this Jesus killer.

CRTSCH
CRTSCH
CRTSCH
CRTSCH
CRTSCH
CRTSCH
CRTSCH
CRTSCH
CRTSCH
CRTSCH
KOTZ
RATSCH
WPKütting 86

Brief Mutter an Sohn

Dear Son:

Thank you for the bottle mail.
The paper is still a little bit brown.
But this is half so wild.
The main-thing is that it stinks not more.
Your father is at home again.
He wants not more wait for the end of the world.
It is really a cross with him!
Every day he is so blue like Enzian.
In his delirium tremens he pisses in ash-trays and shits in the corners.
On Wednesday he was in Hamburg on Aunt Luise's birthday. She told me that he had so a monkey that he threw 10 pence in the park-clock and said:
Shit! Already again 6 pounds more!
And the greatest hammer comes now. Yesterday we had bean soup. When we went to bed he began to fart like a worldmaster. I tell you, it stank so that I could no more breath. I think he is fouling inside.
Then this idiot wanted make scientific test. He wanted find out whether only air comes out of him or whether it is gas. So he lifted his night-skirt over his head, drew his long undertrousers down and told me to light the match when the next fart comes out.
I did so, and since that time he is lying in bed.
On his front side.
Because his ass is full of fire-bubbles.

And it is me a special pleasure to make him compresses with salt water.

Yesterday, your brother and his friend found a dead man before the shimnasium. You know that your brother cannot speak so good and that he stotters a little bit.

And because he was afraid that he cannot speak out the word shimnasium when they bring the dead man to the police, they pulled the cadaver before the post-office. Post he can speak out very good.

So much for today.

P.S. My thumbs are aching from pressing. Have you found this Jesus killer?

Brief Sohn an Mutter

Dear Mother:

I am so very much sad. I run from Pontius to Pilatus to find this bloody killer. But nothing. Jesus Christ, how can I find an man which I have never seen? I think this is no job for me. Jesus Christ??! . . . Jesus?! . . . Mother!!!!! They have assed me!!!
Can you remember? This Jesus was the Hippy who was nailed to the cross five thousand years ago, because he tramped over the water and because he made wonders and so.
He was a revoluzzer who collected the people to follow him. He made evening-meal with them and gave them dry bread and wine.
Our pastor told us the stories one Sunday when they had no freer-beer in the church. He said Jesus was a strong type.
And now I draw my police uniform out and hang this job at the nail. I let me not ass!
Yesterday, I was in the zoo. It was great! They have a lot of wild animals. But the best are the monkeys. They have a large Urang Uttan family.
Papa monkey looks like uncle Adam. Silver-look, a lot of hair, flat nose, too long arms, too large feet and bad teeth. I believe he is the ghost from uncle Adam, and he knows me, because when he saw me he smiled. Just like uncle Adam.
We had a long talk together about old times.
And one of the baby monkeys looks like I when I was 2 years old. Really goldy!!!
When I left the zoo they wanted not let me go because of my fleas. They said I had stolen the flea circus. Mother, you know

that I never steel fleas. You know that I have my own. And I have enough.

It was easy to show them that my fleas are my own. Because they cannot speak English. And they have not a flea with a wood-leg like my Hannibal.

Next week I visit uncle Adam's ghost again.

Now I go to find a new job.

Make it good until next time.

Your Son

Mutter an Sohn

Dear Son:

What is'n that for a police! They are really stupid like bean straw. So what!! That hold you in the head not out.
It is better when you let the fingers from this job. You have it not necessary. You are so a clever boy. You can have what betteres. You can already so good English. That makes you so quick nobody after.
When you go to uncle Adam's ghost in the zoo, tell him that he owes me still 100 East-Frisian dollars. He is a real slit-ear, because he simply threw the towel without giving me my money back. On Monday your father bought a new beißicle. A red one. With alu-wheels and 10-floor.
Yesterday, he drove for the first time in his life. He was full, fuller goes it not. It was a picture for the gods.
First he tried 3 rounds around the house. And 3 times he landed in the cow shit. But he gave not up. He made his eyes free from the cow-shit, drank half a bottle Gin, and then he tried it again from the small hill behind the church.
With a monkey-tooth he stormed the street down. He was not more to stop. On his way, he overrolled the pastor, the postman, 3 pigs, 1 dog, 2 cats, me and our house-door.
Him happened nothing. He landed between the potatoes in the cellar. But the beißicle is hin. Two eigths. Nothing more to make. And the pastor said no free-beer for him on Sunday in the church. That happens him right.
This is enough for today. Make it good.

Your mother

GACK
KLACK
POST
ZIPPP

Sohn an Mutter

Dear Mother:

Thank you for the bottle mail. You are really a poor woman. Your man ist from all good ghosts lost. If he makes so further, throw him in the sea. He cannot swim; perhaps the devil hols him.

Me goes it very good. Mother, imagine, I am now a member of American Express. It is so what from fantastic. I need not more cash money. I explain it you:

They give you a little plastic card with your name. And when you want buy something you must not pay cash money. You only show the card and underwrite a little paper. And then they get the money from the bank.

You can say what you want: America is a very modern country. I have already bought a lot of fine things. 5 shoes, 15 socks, 2 short undertrousers, because it is very warm now.

And a water bed. Because the wood-worms have eaten my old bed. Very good work. And because they don't like the water-bed, they have drawn out. To the door. They make it short and small.

My water bed is really super. But always I have pressure on the pipe because it blubbers and shwabbels so beautiful. But that makes nothing. I have bought a piss-pot for beside my bed.

Tomorrow, I buy a car, because I want not more walk. Me qualm already the socks from so much walking and looking for a good job.

I write you more next week.

Your son

Mutter an Sohn

Dear Son:

Your bottle mail was six weeks underway. This is really a big dog.
Tell this American post-minister that he is a night-cap.
Is it really true that you pay only with a plastic card? I think me kicks a horse. I cannot believe. My inner voice says me that there ist what foul in the state of Denmark. You know: From nothing comes nothing. Wood-eye be careful. I feel it in the urin, this goes not good. Believe your clever mother. The thick end comes soon.
This is so sure like the Amen in the church. I think these Americans have it fist-thick behind the ears. They are all neck-down-cutters.
But do, what you cannot let. But I tell you, it's going in the trousers.
On Sunday, your father and I were in the movable cinema in the neighbour village. We saw a film with Dracula.
Your father, full as always, liked it very much. His eyes were glitzering, and suddenly he jumped from chair to chair to bite the people.
I shamed me so. After 10 minutes, they threw him out. When I came home, he looked at me so funnily that me fell the heart in the trousers.
The next morning I had two holes in my neck und felt very blood-poor.
Since Tuesday, he has a black coffin in the cellar behind the potatoes, with garden soil.

There he sleeps now every night. I let him not more in the sleeping room.
I think slowly he turns through. Next Sunday, they show another film. From Oswald Kolle. Up-clearing. I hope your father will not jump from chair to chair again.
Write me soon back.

Your Mother

Vater an Sohn

Dier san,

Juhr masser säis ei go piepel hei skuhl änd reit ju lätter in inglisch. Ei känn nau Inglisch ghud bat tie-ätsch is schit. Wänn ei spiek tie-ätsch mei tieß fohl aut.
Gous ju guhd? Ei not so.
Juhr masser gif mi nix trink. Schie säi ei ollwäiß kotz ße bed full änd schie mast mäik ewäi. From mie aut schie mast not mäik ewäi.
Ei säi ei newwer mohr kotz in bed. Ei nau kotz in cuck-pot. Schie mast onli kipp aut. Wänn shie hier wot ei säi schie kotz in korner. Ei not anderständ schie so senßibbel.
Sis is ool natscherel.
Sis is leif.
Ei feind jur pullover witch ju mist sri manß. Ei faund ander mei skört wänn ei mi wosch jesterdäi.
Se pastor wont mi not gif frie bier in tschörtsch. Hie säis ei dä-inger fohr efferiwon. Hie is pig-priest. Hie not klier in häd. Ounlie bicos mei dreif-wiehl häd äksident wiß him. Hie is so after-cärriing. Ei mast spiek pauer-wörd wiß him. Ei säi him iff not frie-bier in tschörtsch ei bai njuh dreif-wiehl änd mäik njuh ättäck.
Sänd mi bit mannie fohr wiskie. Ju gud san.
Nau enaff. Mäik it ghud, bat not so often.

Juhr Faaser

ZACK
AUS
ROH
MITTEL
DURCH
KOHLE

Sohn an Mutter

Dear Mother:

Know you why my bottle mail came so late?
The sea-horses were on strike.
But now they work again.
There is really nothing foul with the plastic card. I have bought a car.
A small one. Because I want learn drive before I buy a larger one.
It is really great. You turn the key, give gas, and equal goes it loose.
I have bought an electric egg-cooker. But it is not so good. Even after half an hour the eggs are still hard like stone. Now I use the egg-cooker to make pell-potatoes.

And I have bought a toaster. A toaster is a thing where you put bread in.
And when the bread is brown, it jumps out. But I don't like this bread. I like more to make pomm fritt in it. They jump so beautiful.

And I have bought a special cook-pot – a quick-cook-pot – to cook my stinky socks and undertrousers.
This is a very fine thing. It is always under pressure. It steams like an steam lock.
But the smell is not so good. And it is a little bit dangerous. When the oven is too hot, the cook-pot flies in the air. That happened yesterday.

Now I must buy an new kitchen lamp, cement for the hole in the ceiling, glass for the window and 3 new teeth for my mouth.
Father wrote me a letter. He writes perhaps funny. His English is not so good. But what can you await from a Suffkopp like him.
I have a new job. In a milk factory. I help make cheese. It stinks like my feet.
Enough for today.

Your Son

Sohn an Vater:

Dear Father:

Many thanks for your letter. Your English is not yet so good. I can only read every 5th word.
I hope it goes you good. Don't drink so much. It is not so good for your liver. When you make so further, you will bite in the grass very soon.
It is really pity that you get no free-beer in the church. Perhaps when you pray the father-our before the pastor's house then he will press his eyes to (and his chicken eyes) and give you some beer.
You are me perhaps a spirit-throttle. Always must you drink one over the thirst. Why don't you drink milk or Cola? Or mineral water? You become no louses in your stomach, as you always say.
And when you drink so much, you always fall out of the roll and make the Molly.
And you always make the trousers full because you have through-fall. I think you are lost from all good ghosts.
You should better go in the water and let my poor mother alone.
I send you some dollars for Whisky. Drink you dead and go to hell.

Your Son

Mutter an Sohn

Dear Son:

Since your father has your letter, the hell is loose. I have really nothing more to laugh. He is so angry on you. He wants come over and knock you out. What a luck that he knows not the direction. Slowly I become cold feet. I hold it in the head not out. Every evening I am glad when he falls in his coffin in the cellar. He likes it very much. He says: how you bed, so you sleep. What have you written him that he makes such a theatre? On Tuesday, he took the bible, went before the pastor's house und prayed the father-our 5 hours long.

But I assume he made something wrong. Because suddenly, the pastor came out and threw him on the street. Together with his empty whisky bottle and wet trousers. The pastor told me his pray: Father-our, in the sky / holy is your name
our daily whisky give us today
and don't forget, 2 litres per day are just enough.
And send my wife where the pepper grows,
and send me a younger one, a knacky one.
And punish my son. He is a ass with ears.
And punish this pig-priest, because he
gives me no free bear. Amen.
Father-our, in the sky / holy......

This man has really a screw loose. And he knows still not what was wrong with his prayer. He says prayer is prayer, egal what for one.

So much for today.

Your mother

Sohn an Mutter

Dear Mother:

You have perhaps a man! Nobody wanted him and you had him equal! Tell him to shoot in the wind.
Know you what you can do? Go and buy some long nails. And when he sleeps, nail the coffin to. Is this not a good idea? And when the flood comes, throw him in the sea. But please not in my direction. Then you are him loose.
Last week I was two days in hospital. Because I had a hole in my head. Because I had some troubles with my car. I cannot understand how all this happened. I can already drive so good. The car has no coupling and I must only give gas.
So I drove and drove and drove. And then came a hair-needle-curve. And then I wanted overhaul a truck. I made this special gang in. R like Rally. I woke up in hospital. With a hole in my head. The policeman said that I am a luck-mushroom. Because I was not hurt more.
The truck behind me had pushed me and my car into the show-window of a washery. I paid everything with my little plastic card.
The car is in ass. Full Schrott. Tomorrow I buy a larger one. With a larger Knautsch-zone. And I never more make the Rally-gang in again. I have really had pig.
Yesterday I got a new job. I am now out-thrower in a striptease bar. They say I have the right face and figure for this job.
They gave me a fine uniform. A red one. Because they say my own trousers and pullover are so muddy that they stand from alone.

I have never seen striptease before. A very fine thing. Vow!! Each time they make it, it becomes me quite warm around the heart. It is a feeling like Christmas. Only flying is beautifuller. And now I go in my water bed und dream from the striptease.

Your Son

Mutter an Sohn

Dear Son:

Me falls a stone from the heart that not so much happened to you and that it is only your head. You make perhaps things! You know that driving is very dangerous. Remember your father with his drive-wheel. Next time you must be a little bit more much carefuller.

I am very glad that you have a new job. Now the money rolls again.

But what in three-devil's name is an out-thrower and what to the hell is stripptease? If it is a piggery, then I forbid it you. Piggy things are nothing for my oldest son. You have really gained what betteres.

Last week, your father promised me to become another man. But nothing changed. Yesterday, he told me that he can nothing for it, because the other one drinks too. Know you what? Now he can me crosswise.

Yesterday it burned on the yard of our neighbour. And in the cow stable. The firemen sprayed out of all pipes to save the cows. When the fire was out, no cow was burnt. They were all drowned.

Your father wants to work in a ready-house company. Because they have erection party* every second day.

Write me soon from the stripptease. *Your mother*

P. S. Drive careful with your new car.

* Um keine Mißverständnisse aufkommen zu lassen, sei dem allzu phantasievollen Leser gesagt, daß es sich hier um "Richtfest" handelt.

Sohn an Mutter

Dear Mother:

Thank you for the bottle mail. I tell you what striptease is. It is when girls draw out everything what they have on their body. Everything! Mother, this is a hammer! I have never before seen so many girls in Adam's costume. And everyone can see it! Vow!! Mother, you are right, it is a little bit piggery. But I tell you, I work not more in that bar. Because I threw the wrong man out. He was the boss.

Yes, yes, this is life. But I worry not. I find another job, because I am not fallen on the head.

I have now a new used car. It is much a lot larger then the old car, where the dogs could look through the windows and pissed on the out-puff.

The dealer said the car needs new candles. Can you send me some from the Christmas tree? So I must not buy.

The car has lying seats. I don't know for what. Lying I cannot so good drive.

The wheels have no profile. The dealer said this is very good, because without profile I can drive quickerly.

And what is really great is that there comes so much fresh air through the bottom. Without these holes in the bottom I could not breath. Because of my feet.

Make it good, Mother.

I write you more when I find a new job.

Your Son

"Darling?"
"Yes, my dear?"
"Is it true that people are falling to dust when they have died?"
"Yes, my dear, that's true."
"Then look under the sofa. There are at least three cadavers there!!"

Brief an Ehevermittlung – Mann

Dear Madam Butterfly:

I have seen your address in the newspaper from Monday before one year. You know what? I'm so alone, and now I want to marry. You help me, yes?
I'm a very nice man. Only 36 years old, full black hair, brown eyes, 1 Meter 80 large, no fat. My body is like from Adonis.
I have a beautiful house with many rooms and a garden around the house. I like children, and I want make children now, before it is too late und before it goes not more.
I spend not much money. I save half my dollars on the bank.
I can make everything alone. I can make coffee, I can cook like a young god, I can wash my white under-trousers. All people like me. I can wash up the bottom.
I am very strong. Overall. I can work like a horse. I have good teeth. And I am a very clean man. I wash me every day. Overall. I am never ill.
I send you a picture from me. I am the 10th from the left. I have made a X where I am. But this is only if you cannot count. Have you a woman to marry me? Look in your papers und write me very soon. I want one with a smiling face und which speaks not too much. And which is not so heavy that I can carry her on my hands. I make her early-piece in the morning, I go buying in the town, I make the bed, I make her babies. I make her what she wants. Tell her. She will have it very good. And the devil can hol me if I do not say the naked truth.

Your Mr. Knockout

BRIEF EINER FRAU AN EHEVERMITTLUNG – FRAU

Dear Missis Buterfly,

Now I wait already one year that you find a man for me. Is this so difficult? Thunder-weather! Now it is highest train. I want a man. I want marry.
Want you take me on the arm? I pay not money for nix. Make and find a man for me!
My two childs are also already sour. You have my picture. Don't lay on the foul bear-skin.
You know that I am very attractive woman. But I become not younger. And my money goes slowly out.
I am a perfect house-woman, I can work hard in the garden. And I can make a man happy in the bed. But we can also do it on the carpet on the bottom. I am very flexible, if you know what I mean.
I can go with a man through thick and thin. In bad and good days (I like more the good days).
But I don't want a man who is still wet behind the ears. I want an ripe one. A man who goes out with me and who can dance. A man who likes liver-cheese and spinach (that I can cook best). A man with whom I can live in the seventh sky. A man who drinks not so much alcohol.
Please find so a man for me, because I am so mother-soul-alone with my two children.

Your Mary Pickle-Head

Brief an Ehevermittlung (Mann) nachher

Dear Mrs. Butterfly:

Do you know the speak-word "Love makes blind"? I tell you, I have been blind like a mouth-throw, when I married this Mrs. Pickle-Head with her two spasties. The high-time was quite good.

And she saw quite good out. But the high-time night? Forget it.

First she drew her plastic hair away.

Then she removed the false wimpers, then she put her teeth in the water glass.

And when she had removed the 1 cm make-up from her face, she looked like her name: Pickle-Head. Huhh! Is this woman perhaps ugly! Ugly like the night.

But when I draw her a potatoe bag over the head it is not so bad. I told you that I want a woman which is not too heavy. But she is so heavy that I need a crane to carry her through the door. She must be Mrs. Devil. Every day she makes me the hell hot. She cannot get the neck full. She says taking is better than giving. And every day liver-cheese with spinach!

I told you that I want a woman who speaks not so much. She speaks me a hole in the belly. She speaks so much and so quickly that she has no time to breath. She speaks me the ears off and on again.

And she always wants that I maloch. This goes on no cow-skin. And the children. Ugly as her mother. They are straw-stupid. Cannot count to three. And make noise all the day.

No, this is nothing for me. No early-piece in the morning, every

day liver-chees and spinach, and only work, work, work. The only pleasure I have is to speak with my rabbits.
In cannot make her babies, because it would be a catastrophe to have more of these devils. Tomorrow, I will throw them out, and they can go where the pepper grows.
And you can throw my card away. You will never hear from me again.

Unfriendly greetings.

Luis Knockout

Brief an Ehevermittlung (Frau) nachher

Dear Mrs. Butterfly

First you need over a year to find a man for me and my children. Then you have found one. But what for a one.
I can tell you this is the shock of my life. Me stand the hairs to mountain.
He is not 36 years old. This is an error. He is between 63 and shine-dead.
And he looks like a dry Ginseng-root.
I make what with. He has no house. It is a rabbit stable. And there is no garden. Only a few flower pots around the stable.
I wanted a sky full of violins. And what have I? A foam-beater on earth!
Every day he has one sit. He smokes like a chimeney. He wants not work. He wants push a quiet ball. He makes me the life sour. He has no dollars. Only a wood bank before the rabbit stable.
He has only 4 teeth. Two up and two down. Like a rabbit. He likes not my liver-cheese with spinach. And he says bad words like shit and piggery and so. And he is not so good to my lovely children. They don't like him.
He has so funny eyes. With his left eye he can look in his right pocket. And we go not often in the bed. He wants not make babies. He cannot. Always he wants that I pull a potatoe bag over my head. What mean you, Mrs. Butterfly? Is this a man for me and my children? No Madam. This is a man for somebody who has killed father and mother. But not for me.

He cuts his foot-nails when we sit around the table und eat our midday-meal. When he eats, the sabber runs down his chin.
He makes his trousers full. His nose runs all day and night. No, thank you.
Before I make my hands dirty and bring him around the corner, I take my children and go.
And you and your marriage institute can kiss my backside.

Mary Pickle-Head

P.S. I send you one of his full trousers. Put them to your papers.

BRIEF VERMIETER AN MIETER

Dear Mr. McSpeck:

My wife told me to write you this letter because if I don't write it, she will draw me the noodle-wood over the head.
You cannot imagine how this hurts. I know it, because sometimes when I come home in the middle of the night, she stands behind the door with this murderish instrument and hammers on my head.
You don't know her. She has hair on her teeth, and she has her own razor for her double-chin. Therefore, please, Mr. McSpeck, pay the rent for the last 10 months. My wife says that you must get a lot of children money, you work, your wife works and that you must have money like hay.
Dear Mr. McSpeck, if you don't pay the rent, I have no money to buy what for between my teeth and I must eat vegetables from my wife's garden all the time.
I feel already like a flower cabbage, and the carrots come me already our of the ears. This is really not fair from you. I don't even know how a Schnitzel looks like. And my wife says if you don't pay the rent, I will have to eat vegetables for the rest of my life. Please do me that not on!
My wife says if you don't pay until next week, she will kick the shit out of you. And me. I tell you, I know what this means. I know from experience. She has shoe size 42!! So you should better pay very soon!
Nothing for ungood. *Your Mr. Habeduddel*

P.S. I was wrong. My wife has shoe size 45!!!!!

Brief eines Bayern an die Nasa

Greet God!

I write you, because you must help me. I have seen your Space Shuttle in the television. In color. And so came me the idea to make holidays in the world-room. Alone. Without my crazy wife.
I am the Kraxlhuber. The King of Bavaria was my clock-clock-grandfather.
I stand on a very bad foot with my wife. Always she shouts with me. She has a shrill voice like a circle saw. She lets no good hair at me.
She says I am a Schlapp-tail. She wants that I become Bürger-master. But I want not be Bürger-master. I have nothing at the hat with the political shit. I want my Ruah. And so I want make holidays on the moon. Without my bad half.
But I take my dog with me. He is a boxer. His name is Wurstl.
So Is want book a flight in your next Space Shuttle. But please give me not a window place. I would kotz you the rocket full, because I am not swindle-free. And no standing-place please.
And please do not tell my wife that I want go alone. She has a big Schrot-gun. She would make a sieve from my ass.
I need not much comfort. A nice double-room with bath and kloo and heating. And windows with look to the earth. So I can look through my far-glass and see my wife working on the potatoe field. And I and my dog laugh us a branch (hähä). We will kringel ourself before laughing (höhöhöhö)!
Is what loose on the moon? I need worm weather and I hope the sun shines every day. This is very good for my frost-boils.

I need not much. A good bread-time, a good Hax'n and a Mass beer.
Have they chew-tobacco on the moon? If not, I bring it with. Is in the rocket place for my drive wheel?
Tell the man of the moon that I come. I hope he has no wife. We can make out-flights with my drive wheel. We can make crater-wandering. I bring him the Bavarian national hymn bei.
We can make tobacco chewing. We can drink a lot of hop-blossom-tea. I hope he is no Preiß!!! We can spuck around the bet. We can make finger-hooking.
I bring the Bavarian flag with and we can dance shoeplattler around it.
Have they many flies on the moon? If yes, I bring my weather-frog with. He will get fat like a otter.
I want make 5 weeks holidays. When you have no new rocket after the five weeks, I wait for the next rain-bend and drive with my Radl.
Please make me a good price – under good friends. I cannot pay so peppered prices because my pocket money it not so much.
Send your answer to my neighbour Wastl Hintermoser.
I have the honour.

Your Alois Kraxlhuber.

P.S. Don't fly when is full-moon. My dog, this pig-Bazi, becomes always epileptic and makes so much noise.

BRIEF SÄUFER AN SÄUFER

Hallo, McSuff:

I spent half my money to buy something to write. This do I only for very good friends.
And, you old red-nose, how goes it you? What makes your liver? Is it still working?
My doctor says my liver is like a sieve. He says I make it not more long. Can you immagine that, McSuff? Shitt on this doctor. From now on, I drink over the milt.
I write you because I want invite you. I want go with you on the Inter-Schluck Congress. It is only 20 km from here, and I think we can make it in 5 days.
I have "stripped" a land-card and made a cross where we find the supermarkets with the cheapest sprit. This is verry important for so thirsty souls like we. We can buy all the good things for an apple and an egg.
And when we are on the Congress, we let the pig out. There laughs you the heart in the breast. We will make us all honour.
We need no money on the congress. All the suff is free, because I have two free-cards. Eating must not be. We drink this bit.
They have a lot of fine things. Alko-specialities from the in- and outland, headache pills with cognac-taste, flag killers with onion-taste, schwankometers and watertight undertrousers.
There will be intelligent people who hold speaches about interesting things.

Prof. Dr. Alco Schluckspecht
"Drinking without kotzing –
without training goes is not"

Dr. Prom. Applecorn

"What make you when your boss drinks your whisky?"

Prof. Bommerlundern

"The delirium – a märtyrium"

And then the great finale with ex-and-hopp-drinking!

They have special cells for drinking-stars with more than 4 promilles. I'm sure we get a nice double-cell.

I meet you next Monday in the spirit shop in the King Street. Don't forget the newspapers for underway. It is already cold in the nights under the bridges.

I greet you with a thundering Hick-Hick, Hurrahh!!!

Your schnaps-brother

Mc-Nipp

P.S. Do you know a word without "k"? No? It is quite easy. Alohol. Hä, hä (rülps).

An Gebrauchtwagenhändler

Dear Mr. used car:

You sell me used car. I buy used car. Car cost lot of money.
But car no car. Car shit.
You say car very strong, power motor.
Nix strong, nix power. Only tucker, tucker.
Kruzifix!! I not pay money for Schrott-car.
First drive, left door ab.
Second drive, right door ab.
Nochmal drive, out-puff ab.
Car is no car. Car is Traktor.
Next drive, Rad ab.
Blinker goes, goes not, goes, goes not . . .
Last drive, Lenkrad ab. Fast Kopf ab.
Your car very dangerous say the police.
Only for people which are life-tired.
You not send flowers to hospital.
You send money back.
I send car back.
Sonst Bart ab.

I have the honour.

How to hang a picture up

First you go to your neighbour. No. You go not self. You send your wife to your neighbour to borrow a hammer, a nail and a picture (if you have not one). Your neighbour lives only 500 meters from your house. When your wife comes back, you send her to the neighbour again, because the nail is too short. Then you sit down on the sofa and make a plan. Where want you hang the picture up? In the kitchen? In the bedroom? In the living room? In the cellar?
After much thinking you decide to hang it up in the living room. Now, on which wall want you hang the picture? After much thinking you decide to hang it up at the wall where the 3 meter long and 2 meter high book-shelf stands. You tell your wife to remove the books and the shelf (you cannot help because you have it in the cross). You drink a cup of coffee in the kitchen, because you cannot see how heavy she works.
After two hours, your wife is ready (more fix than ready). Now you tell her to go to the neighbour to borrow a metermeasure and a water-balance.
When she is back you send her again to the neighbour to borrow another nail, because for this large picture you need 2 nails. Now you are almost ready to start. What need you else? Hhmmm . . . Ah, you need a ladder. What, you have no ladder? Hhhmmm . . . No, no, don't send your wife to your neighbour. Maybe he stands behind the door with his gun. A chair goes also. Now you can start. You measure from the left wall side to the right wall side. And then from the right wall side to the left wall side. It must be the same measure. Is it? Fine. Over-let nothing the to-fall.

Now you measure the middle between the left wall side and the right wall side and make a point with the ball-writer. Send your wife to bring you one. She is a real pearl.
Now you measure the wall from the ceiling to the bottom. And from the bottom to the ceiling. Only to be sure that it is the same measure.
But you must measure so, that you are near the point you have made before. Now you measure the middle between the ceiling and the bottom and make a point with the ball writer.
Now it becomes criminell.
You take the water-balance and make a long vertical line through the middle-point which you measured from the right wall side to the left wall side. And then you make a long horizontal line through the middle-point which you measured between the ceiling and the bottom.
Now you have a large cross. And the middle of the cross is exactly the middle of the wall! Phantastic!
But if you don't want hang the picture up in the middle of the wall, all the measuring was for the cat. You must then measure a little bit higher or downer or lefter or righter.
Then you measure the distance from the middle of the left up-hanger of the picture to the middle of the right up-hanger of the picture. Good.
Then you transfer this measure with the ball-writer on the wall. Forget not the water-balance! Now it goes loose! You take the hammer and one of the nails and you climp on the chair at the wall. You hold the nail on the left point and . . . hit your thumb! Shit. You see starlets. Oh pain let after!
When your wife has bandaged your thumb you try it again. You hold the nail on the left point and . . . you wake up in the hospital. Your wife tells you that you have hit the main power cable! Try it again in 4 weeks! You see, it is not so easy to nail a picture at the wall!!

FOR SMOKERS ONLY

I'm going to tell you what chaotic and fanatic people you are!
You like to smoke cigarettes. They taste you. It max you nix that you have lungs like a coal cellar. It max you nix that your breath stinks like from a cadaver. I max you nix that you cough like a dog and spuck like a lama. It max you nix that your fingers and teeth are yellow.
It max you nix that your skin looks 10 years older than you are. You spend a lot of money for cigarettes. You hold it in the head not out, when you have just smoked the last cigarette in the evening and you have not Mark pieces to draw a new pack at the automat.
Do you know what for a work it is to make a cigarette? I tell you.
It begins with tobacco planting in South America or so. When the tobacco leafs are ripe, the whole village runs to the tobacco fields and makes the big harvest. Then the baby tobacco goes on a trip on a ship to good old Germany.
After this long trip the young tobacco is very tired and must sleep. And when it wakes up it is quite ripe. Then they use water-steam to make the tobacco soft. Then the tobacco is mixed with many other tobaccos. And fine things are added. Glycol, aroma, perfume or so, etc. etc.
And now the tobacco comes under the knife. It is cut klitze-small. In 0,7 mm wide stripes. Hhmmm! I can smell it!
Now the tobacco must be dried. Then it is rolled in white paper with or without filter. And now the tobacco is called "cigarettes". Or "Hugos". Or "coffin nails".
Then 20 cigarettes or so are packed in silver-foil and together

with this silver-foil they are packed in a small box. This box ist wrapped in cellophane paper with a special tear-off strip.
The small packs with 20 cigarettes or so are now packed in larger boxes (10 small packs in one larger box). And this large box is also wrapped in cellophane paper with an special tear-off strip.
Now a lot such boxes with 10 packs with 20 cigarettes or so are packed in noch a larger box. Or carton. These large cartons with the lot of large boxes with 10 packs with 20 cigarettes or so are then delivered to the cigarette sellers.
There, the boxes with the 10 packs with 20 cigarettes or so are packed out and the cigarettes are sold in these boxes or the 10 packs with 20 cigarettes or so are sold one after the other.
Now you go and buy a pack of cigarettes. You grip the special tear-off strip und you tear off the cellophane paper.
You open the pack and draw a piece of silver-foil out.
You take a cigarette out, you light it with zittery fingers and . . .
and then you burn and destroy it in say and write FIVE MINUTES!
All the work was for the cat!!! What camels you are!!!
P. S. By the way, I smoke about 50 cigarettes per day!

GEBET EINES JUNGEN

Hi, God!

It stinks me that I must pray to you every day. You are far away from the shot in your sky and you don't know what I make through. You have nothing to do with all this shit here. But I am here alone with my problems with my parents.
Come down and look. They say I am a little devil. But when I am a little devil, why must I pray to you?
They say that you see everything and that you hear everything. When I bore in my nose and make little balls and when I say dirty words like shit and asshole and idiot and fuck you and so, why don't you tell me that this is not quite so good? Have you never said dirty words, are you never sour, drive you never out of the skin?
Don't tell me that you are so brave. That would be a fist-thick lie. I want always be a brave boy. But they let me not. Everything is going in the trousers. I really want wash my ears and brush my teeth. But not so often. How often do you wash you?
They say I always say the wrong things. My father said when my Aunt Isolde comes, the sun goes up, but when she opens the mouth, the sun goes quickly down again. I told my Aunt what he said und she was gone for ever. Was this wrong?
My mother said that Uncle Heini is old enough now to die, because we want to draw in his new villa. I told him that. Last week he made an new testament. I don't know what this is, but it must be very bad, because my father laid me over his knee; I could not sit one week long.
Why is it right when they say such things and why is it wrong

when I say such things? I understand the world not more. There is no justice on earth.
My father told my mother that he had bought a hot Video film. When they were in the theatre yesterday, I made the Video on. It must have been really hot in this film, because all people were naked. And made an big fight. On the bed and on the bottom. Really funny.
My father has a great stamp collection. But totally through another. I put the red ones to the red ones, the blue ones to the blue ones and the green ones to the green ones. And for all this heavy work I took 3 stamps and changed them for 2 white mice, a frog and 5 rain-worms.
When I told my father he flipped out. He sprang in three corner. And then he told me that I would not get pocket money for the next 50 years. Is 50 years very long?
Now I want sleep. I have a hard day behind me. Maybe I pray to you again next week. Or never. Because is brings me nothing. So long.

Gebet eines Mädchens

Dear God!

I am so sad. My mother likes me not more. She says I should pray to you that I become a brave girl.
She says I am the nail to her coffin and that I bring her in the grave one day.
She says I should tell you all the bad things I have done.
Our cat is always running around the gold-fish glass. So I helped here in the glass that the gold-fish is not so alone.
Now I don't know were the gold-fish is, but the cat is very happy. Is this bad?
My mother told me not to say so dirty words. So I washed my mouth with palm-olive because I want that clean words come out.
When my mother saw the foam before my mouth she got a white face and thought I had the toll-rage. But the doctor said it was not and the words then coming out from my mother's mouth were everything else than clean! I cannot repeat.
In the children-garden we have painted with finger colours. Really wonderful. I tried them out at home. On the walls. And on the curtains. On my father's good jacket. On my mother's new hat. On the couch. And on the TV. Because we have only black and white TV. The bill from the cleaning company was not too high. But my mother said that she gets crazy, if this goes so further. Is this bad?
Dear God, you know that I have wunderful marbles*? Last

* ,Murmeln

week I ate about 20 of them. They had no taste. When I sat on the toilet 2 days later, it was very funny. It made klick, klick, klick, klick, klack (this was the biggest one). It took me 2 hours to clean them.

Next week I will try again. With more big ones. Because I like klack more than klick.

This morning, I found my father's cigarettes on the kitchen table. I wanted to smoke one. But I had some trouble with the matches. Tonight we sleep all in a hotel.

In 6 months our new house will be ready, and my new bedroom will have a pre-hang-lock.

Please dear God, make that I become a brave girl, because I want not to be a nail.

Now go to bed and sleep well. And don't forget to pray.